# UnBrokable*

# V

## The 5th 10 Reasons Why People Go Broke Despite Working

Brad Kong

# Disclaimer

These are the full title and subtitle of this book:
***UnBrokable* V: The 5th 10 Reasons Why*** *People Go* ***Broke*** *Despite Working*

I wrote only "***The 5th 10 Reasons Why Broke***" on the front cover *intentionally* for rhyme, simplicity and focus.

The graphic on this book cover is from Edit.org. I use the site to design my covers; it provides book cover templates with its copy-righted images to writers who paid "annual memberships."

I do have three proofs of my membership to Edit.org, payment receipt for the membership through Paypal and reference address to the image of the site. I am writing this because I received emails regarding my "book cover images" twice; both of which were resolved within a day. I decided to stick to my own or edit.org's images since I cannot keep getting copyright emails. If you have any issue regarding my cover art, feel free to contact me: I will be more than happy to provide the three proofs again.

Also by Brad Kong

**UnBrokable* series:**

*Introduction to UnBrokable**
*UnBrokable* I* (Chapter 1 to 10)
*UnBrokable* II* (Chapter 11 to 20)
*UnBrokable* III* (Chapter 21 to 30)
*UnBrokable* IV* (Chapter 31 to 40)

**UnBrokable Preliminary series:**

*Introduction to UnBrokable** (Chapter 1 to 5)
*Intro to UnBrokable* Large Print*

*UnBrokable* I* (Chapter 1 to 10)
*UnBrokable* II* (Chapter 11 to 20)
*UnBrokable* III* (Chapter 21 to 30)
*UnBrokable* IV* (Chapter 31 to 40)
*UnBrokable* V* (Chapter 41 to 50)
*UnBrokable* VI* (Chapter 51 to 60)
*UnBrokable* VII* (Chapter 61 to 70)
*UnBrokable* VIII* (Chapter 71 to 80)

*UnBrokable** (Chapter 1 to 80)

**Brad Short Story Collection I:**

*Robbery at Cyb Knight*
*How to Get Rid of Ladies*
*11 Girls I had Loved*
*Say No To TSLA*
*3 Ways to Avoid Divorce*

*15 Ways to Keep Your Teeth Healthy*
*5 Moments When I Felt Sorry For My Cat*
*Corn Dog Grandpas*
*Condo Chronicle*
*How to Lose 40 Pounds*

**Brad Short Story Collection II:**

*15 Things You Didn't Know About Korea*
*3 Reasons Why We Need to Buy a Home Early*
*Why Are CDs Super Important?*
*Say No To TSLA (2nd Edition)*
*Large Pizza for $5*
*30 Reasons Why I am Great*
*3 Reasons Why the Nursing Home Filed Bankruptcy*
*3 Mistakes Offline  Small Business Owners Make*

**Free books are available all the time!**

1. Go to: https://amazon.com/author/bradkong
2. Filter books by "Price Low to High."
3. Download available free books.
4. Read and please *leave a rating*.

All the books are available free for 5 days every 3 months – read all of them! Enrich and grow your life!

# Praise for *UnBrokable*

"This is the best book I have ever read. I am saying this only because Brad is my husband."

-Tsina D,
A housewife and teacher

"I cannot believe my dad wrote this much thick book. He must be a genius."

-Yuna K,
An elementary school student

"I am proud of my son who wrote a book in English."

-Mrs. Jin,
A wealthy woman

"Publishing this book is a celebration itself. Write your name on the next page if you bought this for a gift."

-Brad K,
A philosopher, writer, publisher, book designer and investor

# Un*Brok*able*

Dear ______________

This book is my gift for you.

It has been helpful for me, so I hope it will be helpful for you as well.  Thank you always.

Sincerely,

From ______________

For All the Honest Workers
Struggling Everyday

# Foreword

So many books out there from Self-Help and Financial Gurus talk about personal finances in abstract terms. These are folks who make millions selling books telling us what to do. Here is something new and refreshing, however. The author relates his real-life experiences in personal finance. Not only is there a lot of good advice in here, it is an interesting look into someone else's life.

It seems we are at a time in history where everyone is struggling to get ahead. But then again, if we look back in history, it has always been this way. The inflation of today pales to that of the 1970's. The unemployment of a few years ago was nothing like that era, either. What is frustrating for so many is that even "making good money" people are living "paycheck to paycheck" and wondering where the money all went. I know I fell into this trap!

The author illustrates how people go broke even while making a hefty salary, and provides a guide to being "UnBrokable" - a term he has coined. And apparently it works - he retired at 40, not from selling self-help books (like so many Gurus do) but by being careful with money.

There is a lot here to learn from. And it's only just getting started!

**Robert P. Bell**
Georgia
USA

Mr. Bell is a retired Patent Attorney, self-made millionaire and founder of "**Living stingy**" blog. He has written in the last 15 years since 2008 and helped tons of people get out of debts and money pitfalls. He is known for his humorous, witty, but sharp writing style and has influenced myriads of writers, including Brad Kong.

# Contents

66. Being Unlucky
67. Not Solving Housing Problems Quickly
68. Much on Ceremonies & Anniversaries
69. Not Using Infrastructure Already Built
70. Not Working While Being Wealthy

***UnBrokable* VIII***

71. Going Too Big
72. Not Being Awake
73. Too Fantasizing Wealth
74. No Long Term Vision
75. Being Deceptive
76. Being On the Wrong Side
77. Not Going Straight to "Profitable or Not"
78. Having Low Self Esteem
79. Not Being Constructive
80. Not Having Enough Room to Breathe

# Prologue

*Dying poor is a shame, especially in wealthy countries.*
*It is not all about money– it shows how we have lived.*
-Brad Kong

This is me sitting on the Ferrari in Miami, FL in 2003 – a rich boy spending his parents' money lavishly. Then, I didn't expect I would go broke abysmally and suffer for a decade.

Hamas from Palestine attacked Israel in October 2023. A war broke out and over 6,000 people have died so far in the past month. I am not sure of anti-Zionism, but if I were Israelis, I wouldn't have tried to expand my territory against Palestinians. Technically, **the land of current Israel doesn't have much commercial values – no oil, agriculture or water resources.** I would try to keep some lands near Tel Aviv, which is over 10 times bigger than Hong Kong or Singapore, and try to build a new city like Dubai there. I wouldn't have fought over useless lands with Palestinians, who have been long-term dwellers; I would rather let them keep most of it as I need what I need. **The fact that we don't think practically can be a reason to be poor.** *Land used to have "absolute values"* in agricultural societies, but that's an *old concept*, not applicable any more. Also, I wouldn't stick to Jerusalem necessarily, only because my ancestors lived there millennia ago. The *point* is to obtain safe land for Jewishes to settle; 80% of Australia or Canada are virtually empty now. I wonder what Moses would do if he governs now – by the time he led the Exodus[1] out of Egypt, North America was not even discovered yet.

Jack Whittaker was a construction company owner in Putnam County, WV – best known as the winner of a lottery jackpot of $315 million in the Powerball in 2002. He was a millionaire already with a net worth of $17 M even before winning – in a word, a rich man won a bonanza. Oddly enough, a series of unfortunate events happened to him afterwards. First, a guy named Tribble, the boyfriend of Whittaker's granddaughter Brandi, was found dead of drug overdose in Whittaker's home in 2004; three months later, Brandi herself was also found dead at the age of 17; cocaine and methadone were found in her body. Five years later, Bragg, who was Whittaker's daughter and the mother of Brandi, was also found deceased at 42 in Daniels, WV. Then, Whittaker's home in Bland County, VA, was reported

[1] 1,400 B.C.

to be on fire in 2016. Finally, Mr.Whittaker himself passed away following a long illness at 72 in 2020: *Why did the luckiest guy in the world pass away earlyish after losing all his children?* I am not a Jewish or Muslim, but I turned 50 this year. The best thing I am glad about is that I haven't drunk or smoked for life; I have been aware that my body is the only thing I have. I am relieved that I didn't damage my organs more, though my kidneys and teeth are somewhat impaired by drinking sodas for decades.

Han Liu was a Chinese billionaire, the former chairman of Hanlong Group in mining businesses. His assets were claimed at $6 billion USD by the time he passed away at 49 in 2015. He was convicted of murdering 8 people and running a mafia-style gang for his business; he was executed by the law enforcement in China. His last words had been viral: "Life is short; *we don't have to live too diligently for more money.* I will have a small store and live happily with my family next life."

These three episodes gave me some lessons: we don't have to work to death, make a lot, spend more and leave a fortune to others; I do not want to *grind* myself to donate more. In *Psychology of money* by Housel, there is a story of a man named Read, who had been a janitor for 42 years, made a fortune out of blue-chip stocks, left $8 M to a hospital and passed away. I know a similar case of Groner, who had worked as a secretary for 43 years, made profit out of the Abbott shares, left $7 M to a college and died. They were undoubtedly honorable. But, seriously, *what's the point?* What would be the thing they regret the most? As long as I have enough, I conclude that **the best reward I can give to myself is *working less.*** I may not need a luxury vacation, but I like to save myself from drudgeries.

Have you ever been a dishwasher before? **If you don't fully agree with this book, it's possible you might not have been broke enough.** I believe a way to be *adequate* is staying away from the reasons causing poverty. Coincidentally, I was in Chinatown Chicago the other day; it had some Korean shops, which were crowded. It took forever for Korea to be wealthy, but ironically, once its people became affluent, they made money out of the fact: *Being prosperous can be a source of income itself.*

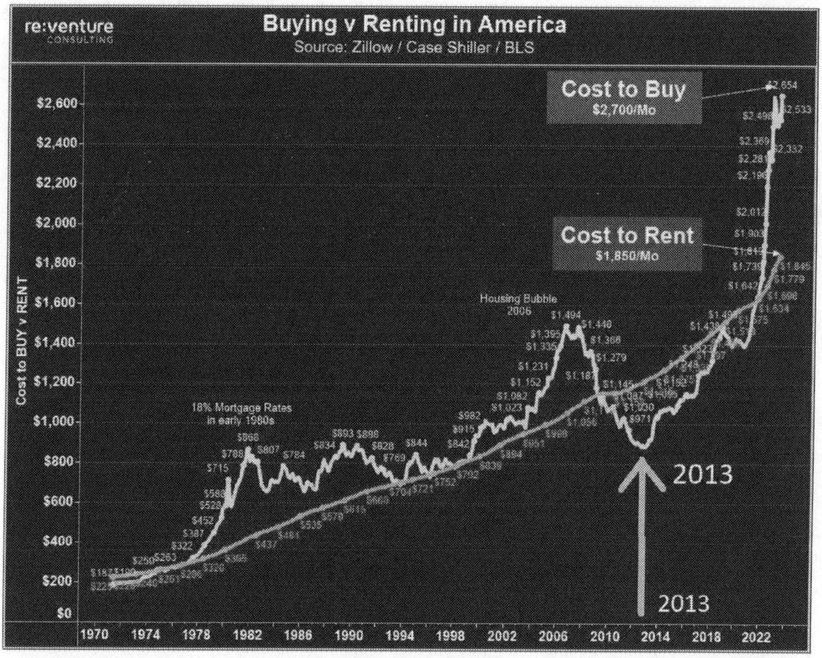


I bought my home in November, 2013. I didn't know it was the lowest price ever in the 21st century (source from Zillow).

My net worth has been up 8 times in the past decade. I had $80,000 CDs in the bank in 2013 – how do I recall it? I bought my condo in full cash of $60,000[2] that year; my real estate agent asked me to submit proof of funds in advance; I didn't know what to do, so I got a receipt from the ATM and gave it to her. Now I have over a $650,000 portfolio, not including my residence, as of 2023. This growth has probably been from inheritance, investment gain, salaries and frugality. But I would say that "not having rent or mortgages" played the most crucial role.

I enjoyed my life until I couldn't. And some of us may not since a recession is looming closely. Maybe this book is not for the super-rich, the middle-class or even mildly poor. I had been in deep destitution, especially around 2009. My business got slow as the subprime mortgage meltdown broke out; my car was a decade old and horrible mechanics kept overcharging me amid anguish; then my daughter was born in 2010. I couldn't waste even a single cent for long, but I was able to manage to buy a small condo thanks to my parents; the only advantage was all the housing prices collapsed, due to foreclosures caused by the heavy depression. This series is written for those: **Unlucky people who have no idea how to get out of poverty.** The Ferrari photo above was taken 20 years ago; then, I had no idea how much trouble I was about to go through. Now I know being wealthy is a combination of

[2] It was low due to the economic depression then.

persistence, knowledge and *luck*. On the contrary, being broke can happen easily for any reason any time.

* * *

Charles Bukowski (1920 – 1994) was an American poet nicknamed "the laureate of low-life" in the 1970s; he bought his first house 23 years *later* than me. His net worth was over $4 million by the time he passed away: How did it happen? Bukowski was occasionally considered a drunk loser, but I found out that he and I share a few things in common. Firstly, we both started writing careers after our 40s; both had or have one daughter. We both had worked for low-waged physical jobs; both inherited some money from parents after becoming middle-aged. Also both were born in foreign countries, originally. Yet it shows that *Buk* bought his first house with a mortgage at 58 in 1979; I bought my condo in full at 40 in 2013. It took an extra 5 years for him to pay off the mortgage, so he ended up buying his house 23 years later than me: What delayed him so long?

It is natural if someone goes broke when he or she does not have a job. But some *go broke* despite working full-time. More ironically, some live wealthy without having a job: *How?* My mother was originally from a poor family (typical for old Koreans) and never had a real job. But she has been in the top class most of her life: What happened? This *UnBrokable** will be a practical and unorthodox guide to stay away from *brokeness*; we will talk about unique reasons, examples and facts, including my memoir. FYI, ***brokeness*** (not broke**nn**ess[3]) is a noun meaning **"the characteristic of not having enough money."**

Have you ever been broke before amid working? Have you been short despite having a full-time job? People may not get broke automatically, especially in wealthy countries; if some are needy despite working to death, there must be reasons. **What does make a person poor?** *Why do some still rent an apartment after working 12 hours a day for 30 years?* I had witnessed a couple of those closely for 7 years. **UnBrokable*** may not be a word in a dictionary yet as I coined it – it means **a person who cannot be broke financially** – it's the opposite of *Les Miserable.* I think it is a misconception that, "If we work hard, we will be rich." It's far from the truth; *in fact,* I believe *working longer can make us poorer;* some live painfully by exploiting themselves that way. I am a middle-aged man with a wife and daughter from the Midwest and my American life can be divided into four periods since 1999.

1. Colleges: Cornell and SUNY at Buffalo (1999-2005)
2. Business: Cyb Knight Video Games (2006-2014)
3. Employment: A nursing home (2015-2022)
4. Investor and writer (2022 - current)

Or I can divide the 24 years by jobs:

- College banquet (2001 - 2002)

---

[3] *Broke**nn**ess* means "a condition in which something is badly damaged."

- eBay Power seller (2003 - 2015)
- Cyb Knight Owner (2006-2014)
- Nursing home dishwasher (2015-2022)
- Investor and writer (2011-current)

I earned two American licenses along the way: medical coder and pharmacy technician. Plus, I have worked for myriads of small jobs since high school: convenience store clerk, bar kitchen helper, military soldier, etc.

* * *

Out of all those jobs, the recent *weekend dishwasher* gave me the inspiration to write *UnBrokable** series. The nursing home I worked at is within walking distance from my home. I had a chance to volunteer to work there one day in 2015; unexpectedly, it brought me a permanent weekend position. Then, I had not done anything for a year after closing out my store permanently in 2014. At the end of the work, they suddenly "wondered" if I could do the job at least every weekend. Now I see the reason why as I asked similar questions to others myself; nursing homes always need employees, while no one is excited to work there. Since they suggested a reasonable pay rate and plenty of free food from the kitchens, I accepted their offer. I had the job only on weekends for six years and on Sunday for a year, close to seven years in total.

I never liked the job since it was physically hard, but I have to admit that it was helpful for my life. First, I had chances to meet a lot of people I would have not without it; there are types of people doing dishwashing for life. Nothing wrong, but I think I was able to see some reasons why they got stuck – **reasons for keeping them in chains.** I think I had enough moments to take a look at their lives; some were *truly great* guys, though. Secondly, the job had brought me physical strength and weight loss, especially in the beginning. Thirdly, the weekend extra wage, bonus and free food still helped me build up my savings faster. There could be millions of reasons why some go broke: gambling, addictions, accidents, etc. **Nonetheless, there are others apparently not doing anything wrong, but always ruined despite working**; many have nothing left after some payments withdrawal at the end of month.

* * *

Do you know when I had the hardest time with money? While I owned the video game store, my daughter was born in 2010. When a baby is born, parents need more money while physically exhausted. Incidentally, the mortgage bubble burst[4] in 2008 and severe depression came from 2009. I guess businesses must have a hard time these days as COVID has been since 2020. While I had wasted my parents' money again only to keep my store open, the only good thing I did was buying a condo in full. Since the economy collapsed in 2008, there had been plenty of foreclosures, short sales and discounted houses on the market – getting rid of rent and mortgage for good was the only upside during that era.

[4] The subprime mortgage crisis.

After being in destitution myself and watching others struggling, I started wondering what really makes workers in trouble: **Is there any *practical trap* making full-timers broke even in wealthy countries?** While working in the nursing home, I saw dishwashers still renting apartments even after *30* years of employment. They occasionally worked *double*, meaning staying up to 15 hours a day: Where did all their money go? Are you ready to jump into 80 chapters with thousands of examples now? **All the episodes are either from my life or true events throughout history.** By the time we reach the epilogue, I hope that we will be more mature, knowledgeable and close to wealth.

# 41

# Too Thirsty for Cash

*Cash can make us impatient,*
*which causes significantly "less" profit in the end.*
-Brad Kong

Baron Rothschild was a German Jewish banker, who was the founder of the French branch of the Rothschild family group in the 19th century. Originally, as a starter, it shows that he was looking for a chance to get acquainted with French high societies to stabilize his operation. He learned those people, so called in leisure class, were bored to death then. Therefore, he hired the best architects to redesign his mansion and chefs to prepare lavish banquets; he threw some cash to hold parties for French elites on a weekly basis; eventually, it says he was able to settle his businesses well.

The similar case was Lorenzo Medici in Florence, now a part of northern Italy, in the 15th century. History says that the Medici family was the absolute billionaire bankers then. To relieve jealousy from the poor, he founded dozens of art schools; even Michelangelo and Da Vincci were students who attended those once. He released some cash to the public this way and it eventually introduced the boom of the Renaissance era later on; it has brought so much money from travelers to Italy even these days. Some people make less money because they go crazy for "cash," which is an instant gain, instead of choosing profoundly lasting assets like real estates, royalty, etc. Some lose money or even lives because they stick to quick profit too much. Let me give you an example from *The 48 Laws of Power* by Greene.

There was a fraud named Count Lustig in America in the early 20th century. He visited Al Capone one day, who was the notorious kingpin, in Chicago in 1926. He boldly suggested, "Mr. Capone. If you give me $50,000, I will double it for you in 2 months." Capone had too much cash surplus temporarily, so he decided to take a risk giving it to Lustig. Then, this shyster put the money in a security deposit box in the bank and did not touch it; he just got it out and revisited Capone a couple of months later. There he said, "I am sorry, Mr. Capone. I was not able to double it. Here is your original fund back." He returned the bundle of bills politely.

Then, do you know what happened? Surprisingly, Capone said, "Wait a minute... You could have run away with this $50,000 bucks? You are an honest guy! We just cannot find a person like you any more. Here is a 10% of my personal gift to you; don't insult me by not taking my appreciation!" Lustig humbly accepted the $5,000 reward from the mob boss. Still, you know what, though? The $5,000 was the profit Lustig was aiming for, from the start, which must have been worth $50,000 in 2023 – quite a large sum of money. Lustig could have lost his life if he got blinded and ran away with the "fifty grand" belonging to the godfather. He ended up being a perfectionist with the impeccable crime since he wasn't anxious for a quick fortune; instead, he was aiming for a smaller amount of gain.

* * *

I decided not to be too stingy one day last year. I read this in a book by chance: "Today is the moment we are truly living: **It is the life of life.**" I decided not to save money blindly – only for later – as I have done in the past decades. It is crazy if I go for more cash forever; this desire for more will be endless. There is a Korean American artist named David Choe, who is best known for his graffiti and mural arts. In 2005, one of Facebook founders, Sean Parker, asked him to paint murals in the interior of Facebook's Silicon Valley office. Subsequently, in 2007, the current FB CEO Zuckerberg commissioned him to paint more murals for their next office.

After finishing all the artwork, it's said that Zuckerberg gave Choe a couple of payment options: "Would you like to get paid by $60,000 *cash* or Facebook stocks of that amount?" A little oddly, Choe chose the stocks even though the company was virtually nameless back in 2007; later, he confessed that he did it by strong suggestion of Parker. Here is the *shocker,* though: When Facebook was listed at the stock exchange[5] in May 2012, **the value of Choe's shares was close to $200 Million.** He suddenly became a mega-millionaire out of a 60 grand job.

Choe could have ended up with a few bucks. I personally took a lesson from this case, as this painter is a Korean similar to my age: "**I will choose something other than cash from now on as long as I have enough savings.**" I assume there are a lot of chances out there, but frankly, I have not had much luck with most of them. *Maybe I have pursued cash too much*; I guess I have been closer to moderate than rich since I have been *too obsessed with* "profits."

* * *

We can see McDonald's everywhere in America now; in fact, it has over 40,000 locations worldwide, as of 2021. It was 1954 when the blender salesman, Ray Kroc first met Richard and Maurice McDonald brothers who founded the restaurant originally in 1940. I actually watched the movie *Founder*, which shows that Kroc was initially a milkshake-mixer salesman. He did not make much sales in the beginning, but was impressed that McDonald's ordered eight blenders all at once, so he decided to visit the joint himself. Fast forwarding, Kroc decided to buy out the whole restaurant locations from the brothers eventually. The two brothers asked $2.7 Million from Ray ($1 M sales profit for each after tax); it

[5] $38 a share, then.

was paid full by Kroc in the end since he was able to raise that much fund successfully in 1961.

What is astonishing here, though? I watched a CBS program showing that Jason McDonald, who is the grandson of Dick McDonald, visited one old Mac location in 2017. This is what he said on TV: "There was 'one deal' on their contract that has never been delivered. Kroc was supposed to pay McDonald family 0.5% royalty from the company profit every year; that would have been worth $100 M a year now. The two grandfathers focused on the quick $1 M cash each and completely forgot about it; that was crazy."

Do you see the aftermath I am trying to display? Those two brothers stuck to only cash in 1961, so they are losing $100 M a year now. **If they chose "something other than cash"** like stocks or loyalties, **they could have been much wealthier** even for generations. We all make this kind of mistake – cash makes our eyesight shorter, narrower or blind.

I have been interested in money making for my whole life, but I have not made that much. Strangely, I have never been interested in marriage much, yet I met a wonderful wife and my family life is fine now. **I feel I have not made much since I have been possessed by money**; in fact, this seems to happen in every field. In the case of stock investment, following financial news closely can be the reason for losses; some are so eager to make money, so they do not see bait from the media; it is secretly known that big corporation scoundrels leak false info into the media to take advantage of small mass investors.

Occasionally, women, who are too keen to get married, do not catch the true face of male abusers: Quality men tend to have high standards, so don't approach many women; when things are too good to be true, I guess it probably is. People skip to see the real values, especially when they are obsessed with anything, including money; I think some of those end up making less or losing it all, afterwards.

* * *

## Summary

1. Unless you are in financial trouble, see if you can choose "something other than cash" if there is a choice of payment.
2. Don't think about money all the time, which is the reason why some people don't make it.
3. Don't put yourself in a financially desperate situation by getting into debt, to begin with; debtors lose the most overall.

# 42

# Smartphone Addiction

*"Cell" phones – we are all prisoners.*
-Brad Kong

There was an openly-gay boy working in the dietary care of the nursing home I used to work at. While I didn't know him well, I knew many people didn't like him much since he was rude – especially for his way of using his queerness to offend others. FYI, I have nothing against gay, particularly; *Sapiens* by Harari is the book I try to imitate and Mr. Bell, who wrote the foreword of this book, may be gay, which I don't care about. I am still not sure where the boy's attitude was from; regardless, he had been close to a lot of female employees. When a male coworker was interested in a girl, he pretended to flirt with the girl in front of him *intentionally* – *indecent* acts in my opinion. Most guys didn't even know if he was homosexual or not: Who cares? He was nobody, anyway. Nonetheless, those got offended for no reason or even got heart broken by his actions. There was a bratty lass close to him, and she and he vexed a lot of people together until both quitted.

Coincidentally, the boy turned out to be a mendacious worker; he checked his phone all the time during working hours. I recall he had an expensive phone and drove a new Corolla his mother bought for him, which was less than 6 months old. I know some may drop phones and get screens smashed, but something much bigger happened to him. When I browsed Facebook one day, I saw a photo of him showing bloody scratches on his arm. It's written that he got in a*n accident* on I-290 and *his car rolled over several times* till it got totaled; apparently, it was damaged beyond repair, so abandoned. To me, it was sort of impossible to have a crash on the spot, especially during summer; it was a wide highway near Woodfield, around where I've never seen a wreck in the last 17 years. **I presume he probably checked his phone while driving.** He could have been dead before becoming 25. Or at least, he blew out a $25,000 new car unnecessarily. The damage caused by smartphones is *bigger than mere internet addiction*; it's estimated that 23% of car collisions involve cell phone use – 1.3 million crashes a year in America.

I thought it was only me in the beginning. Weirdly, I've always felt Latin Americans check their phones more during working. Then, one day, I heard my wife say the same thing. There were a couple of times I had to wait in line longer since the cashiers keep checking their phones in the stores; I don't understand why their managers allow it. I saw many checking it while driving, as if they get paid for *every glimpse.* I personally *never carry* my phone outside home, mostly not to check it longer as browsing hurts my eyes and brain. *Ironically,* I have never lost my phone that way in the past decade.

* * *

There is a Korean celebrity named Yu; unusually, he has been married nine times and two of them were Mongolian women; oddly, he has only 5 wives out of 9 marriages since he had been married to the same women two or three times. He said that he must marry if he is in love, so the ladies can get benefits out of him *legally*. I disagree with him as I have been married *only once* and she is the mother of my daughter. Still, here is *something refreshing* I remember from his interview. When the reporter asked him to give the last words to his fans, he answered, "Just go out." He continued, "You will go crazy if you stay in front of a screen too long." As I heard it, I suddenly felt like he was sane. Wasting time on browsing online is an issue all of us need to deal with; smartphones only extend the waste, which can cause physical accidents, including deaths. *Control is the key*, but alternatively, we can downsize it, at least. I decided to stick to the basic LG smartphone provided for free, so my usage can be limited.

Extended browsing is one way to make ourselves exhausted for nothing. Chronic fatigue from endless checking makes us too tired to do anything. I believe the best way to get out of an addiction is "delaying" or "deterring." First of all, I suggest you see if you can live without the internet at home at all; some use it only at work or libraries, and that's enough for them. In my case, our local library offers 5 hours of free internet a day with their newish computers; if we bring our own laptops, we can use them for up to 12 hours a day. If you need to keep the internet at home, see if you can choose the package of minimum speed with the lowest cost, which should be enough for business use. Strangely, I experienced the faster internet made me browse longer.

For smartphones, see if you can leave it at home when out; this can cut our browsing time literally in half; it may sound overwhelming to some, but personally, I have not detected any problem so far to do so. *Do not keep yourself worn out all the time.* I have lost a lot of things outside in the past decade: an umbrella, four winter gloves, even a backpack, etc. But I have never lost my phone, which is still in mint condition after using it solely at home for 6 years. Also, see if you can choose *free* phones coming with an annual plan. Sometimes, I am forced to stop browsing since my battery gets low easily. I think expensive phones with longer batteries make us more addicted.

I personally have a consistent habit of keeping writing online, which may be a little better than social media addictions; an example of the sites I write is *Reddit*, yet still, there are plenty of similar sites from Korea. I always write my own articles with my own ideas; maybe I have improved my skills a little bit that way in the last twenty years. But I have suffered enough from annoyances by trolls and waste so much time arguing with them, which has absolutely no point. Writing articles *for free* online did not bring me any monetary gain, after all.

I always leave my smartphone at home. Rarely, I bring it out only when I truly need it for double authentication for financial sites when I use a computer at the library: stock brokerages or banking. After entering my user ID and passcode, they usually send a security text to my phone to type in. Other than that, I use my phone as if it is a landline at home, which I had by 2018. I had a mobile phone before only until 2009, but I canceled it since I had never really used it. More importantly, I did not want to get bothered all the time; my wife used to call me anytime when I had it, and we had arguments about it; I thought it's unnecessary fighting on top of spending extra on phone bills. There was *no urgency* to call each other with my wife every few hours. I still had a video game store by 2014 and the store's landline was more than enough.

* * *

There are a few critical advantages when leaving smartphones at home. First of all, we do not have to worry about losing it. I lost an expensive umbrella in 2020, which I believe was left at a Korean restaurant in an impoverished area; somebody must have taken it before I returned there; it was an eatery located inside a supermarket near Belmont Ave in Chicago. On top of it, I had lost my gloves four times in the past two years; I left them once in a bus, and I don't even remember what happened to the other three pairs. Secondly, I can keep my phone in mint condition since I use it only at home – no crack on the screen or anything.

My phone is a free LG android, which I got when I started a year-long contract with Tracfone. I recommend the Mexican company since it has never raised the monthly fee for the last 6 years; AT&T hiked their monthly price every single year, which was the reason why I canceled my service with them. Regardless of costs, things will get complicated if I lose my smartphone somehow. I don't even know how to access brokerages with a new phone; besides, I may have to let everyone know my new number, which is an extreme hassle. In my opinion, the damage caused by a smartphone has three categories: **physical damage**, including death, **lowering vision** and **mental distraction**, which can be lethal. I already talked about the "physical damage" that happened to the nursing home mate above.

As far as "vision damage" goes, as a middle aged man, I must say that I hardly ever got any vision check up in the last 15 years. My vision had never really changed, which is normal or at least, I didn't notice any change, personally. As AT&T kept raising phone bills each year, finally my landline got more expensive than mobile in 2018; it was $29 a month while Tracfone mobile was $16 a month including 500 MB data for the internet. So I switched to Tracfone that year.

But, suddenly, my vision has become more and more near-sighted after that. I think one reason is the distance between my eyes and the screen has gotten much nearer. When I had checked the internet only with a computer, the distance to screen from my eyes would have been about 30 inches (80 cm). Now it has become like 10 inches (25 cm) since I have the phone in my hand and the screen is small. Besides, the screen keeps shedding lights on my eyes, so they get more tired and itching. I changed the brightness of the screen to the lowest and downloaded Gabor eye training[6] app on my phone for now.

Lastly, using more internet via phone has made me more impatient somehow; attention span has been getting noticeably shorter. In a sense, checking the internet is like giving ourselves more work; our body never takes a break as a result. When I close my eyes and meditate, I feel bored, yet **it gives me true rest.** I am glad I have a strict policy to leave my phone at home. Who knows how many times I could have lost my phone? I may be an internet addict, but luckily not a phone addict. Do not give yourself one more thing to carry. We have lots of burden already. Don't give yourself extra work to do. If you cannot control it, just throw it out. Cut the subscription off and save money. See if you can use the internet only at your work or library. It will give you veracious freedom!

* * *

## Summary

1. Browsing a smartphone can do physical harm, including death.
2. Having the internet at home may not be necessary for everyone.
3. If you cannot eliminate those, make your life hard to access them.

[6] This eye exercise game is supposed to improve my vision.

# 43

# Lack of Alone Time

*Time to be alone is minutes to grow.*
-Brad Kong

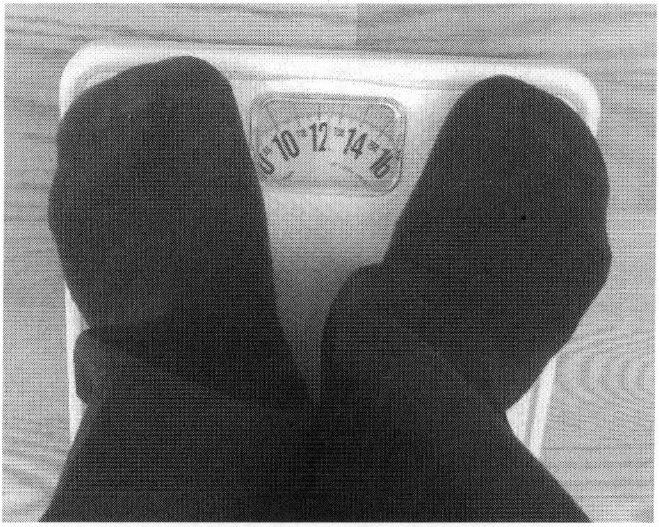


I am 123 pounds in 2023.

The German philosopher Schopenhauer, whose writing style I try to imitate, had been single for life. The first "mademoiselle president" in Korea, Park has never been married, either. Myriads of great minds and over-achievers have been singles. I believe *time to be alone* is *moments to grow* – being able to acquire hours to get solitude is the key to success. People are getting *busier for nothing* these days: Literally, **90% of what we are doing** these days **has nothing to do with survival.** People naturally think being busy is productive, which is misguided. *Often being busy is just being occupied* – nothing more than that. Actually, being engaged for no obvious productivity is a waste.

I watched my frequent Buddhism channel on YouTube the other day. A lady asked the monk why people are still busy in 2022, despite all those technological advancements. He answered that probably "working *two hours a day"* should be enough for basic needs nowadays. He continued, "Koreans were industrious when GNP[7] was $3,000 a year in the 1970s; they are hectic now, even though the GNP is over $30,000 in 2023; they will be manic even if GNP will be $100,000 later." **He pointed out that people keep inventing things to make themselves frenetic.** I understood it as humans are *wired* that way – doing a thing all the time whether it is necessary or not. I think it is important to understand our instincts and need to go against them if that's necessary.

I think that time to *fast* is the true time to take a break. Quirkily to some, we can take breaks from our eating. When I think about it, ingesting food is a lot of work, especially when we need to prepare to cook. I have been 125 pounds in the last few years, but I try to make it down to 120 Lbs. I had a minor jaw infection caused by

---

[7] Gross national product is the amount of money a person can make a year in a country.

a rotten molar tooth, which was extracted last year after four years of recovery attempt; now I am trying to cure possible infection in my mandible completely. I take herbal antibiotics, but believe one way to get rid of the remainder of wicked bacteria is fasting. Losing weight means our bodies eat parts of our own bodies – **they eat diseased cells and germs first.**

* * *

Today I found a news article about a Thai man having two wives and nine kids; his name is Nuttayothin, who is 42, living in Bangkok; it reads he originally had a wife with three kids, but she passed away, unfortunately. He married twice more afterward and all three wives wound up having three kids respectively, so he has nine children total in 2022. Honestly, I have never envied a person having lots of kids; I have been jealous of a big shot having more money or a wordsmith who has written more books; occasionally, I used to begrudge an employee working for a less painful job. But I've never grudged people having multiple divorces or marriages, not to mention countless kids.

Raising a child is a huge obligation from a view; I cannot even take care of my own daughter fully, so frankly, my wife does most of the job now. For the same duty reason, I've never envied a prisoner getting a sentence or a soldier having plenty of years left to complete his or her service. The Thai guy was an auto parts salesman in Bangkok, which is a boiling city with air pollution; he evidently looked painful in the photos. *The worst part of his life* would be *being occupied all the time* – he won't have much time to be alone, which I believe is necessary for both happiness and growth.

* * *

What I didn't like about my mother is she never respects my boundaries; I am 50, but still she always violates it if we have a second to confront.  I don't even know why she keeps calling me while I never call her; I strongly hold every relationship should be mutual, even for families.  It's an old story, but I don't think I had a terrific childhood with my parents in general.  I understand they did their best to raise two kids, who were me and my brother, in infernal conditions; I get it as a father.  But that does not mean I want to get close to them, which I like to say to my mother: "Do not contact me unless I do; as grown ups, the communication ought to be mutual; at least, it should be something like, if I contact you once, you can do it twice.  If I don't forever, you need to accept it as a result of misbehavior for decades."

I didn't have a good time when I was in the army or the nursing home as well.  However, the difference is these places never contacted me again.  I had bad customers when I owned my business; I do not have to see them again.  They also may not be interested in meeting me, but at the same time, they happen to respect my privacy and boundaries.  Or maybe they just don’t have my contacts or whatever. Whenever I hear the voice of my mother, I feel like I am revisiting unpleasant memories from my childhood or young adulthood I wish I could check out forever. She thinks she's doing me a favor by contacting me *first*, which is an absolute misunderstanding – these were nothing but plainly rude acts of invasion. I am never a shy person who cannot contact someone first if I need to.

There was a Thai restaurant waitress. No big deal, but I found a Thai cafe in a village by accident and ate lunch there; then, there was a waitress. She was not outstandingly pretty and it wasn’t an upscale restaurant. But I thought she looked interesting to talk to, so I left her my name and phone number. I don't know if she will contact me or not, but here is one thing for sure: I will never contact her unless she does it first (more likely, I do not have her number in this case). It is not like I don't know how to address people. It seemed she worked so hard to make a minimal living; certainly, she looked bothered when I tried to talk to for a second. I sensed she might have her own issues there, so I left quickly.

* * *

**Summary**

1. Being busy doesn’t mean being productive.
2. Doing anything not to get bored is merely an animal instinct.

3. Poor people often don't acquire enough time to think alone to grow.

# 44

# Not Simplifying

*Having less makes our heads clear.*
-Brad Kong

Some large restaurants focus on only one menu.

There is a novel titled “When life gives you Lululemons” by Weisberger; its main story line is a divorce battle by a spouse of a senator and his model wife, owning three houses. Amid their process, their lawyer found so many unpaid bills in the family: cable, electricity, insurance bills, etc – all either unpaid, overdue or even paid twice. I thought it’s odd in the beginning since that hardly happened to me; maybe it’s because I have only one condo, a wife and a child. When I thought about it, that could be feasible when a family has multiple properties, its husband has numerous partners or the couple doesn't communicate with each other. Obviously, not paying bills punctually can cost an arm and leg in the end.

In that sense, do you know how we can simplify things more than even owning a house? Keeping one place *for life.* By the time I bought my condo 10 years ago, I didn't expect to live here for good. I thought I would buy a small place "in full" *only to avoid rent and mortgage.* But now I suspect I may have to live here longer as a totally different reason submerges. My daughter is in junior high now and by the time she enters college, I may start my "world navigation" – ideally traveling two to three months a year as I get older. I may stay in Korea for two months or visit Angel Falls, Venezuela for a month. However, when I think about it, it's hard to leave a house empty for months that way; a condo would be more consummating for that purpose. Can you see my point here, though? If I live in *a residence* for life *for any reason,* I can maximize my profit as Buffett did; I make and save the largest amount out of it, which has tripled already in the past decade. I can save an enormous sum for not buying and moving into a bigger house.

Do you know how to finish a lot of work in a short time? My personal secret is *simplification.* "Pyon Pyon Sha" is a popular Korean noodle house in Japan; it's said this restaurant gets about 800 customers a day on average; still they manage everything fine with two dozens of staff: How? The eatery has basically only one menu called *Morioka Reimen,* which is traditional cold noodle from the Korean peninsula. Usually, struggling restaurants have dozens of dishes on their menus – as a result, things are getting crazier in the kitchens, while profits are getting shorter.

I mostly order only one dish and try to finish it completely whenever eating out. I notice that some order diverse menus and don't really finish them all, which is wasteful. Simultaneously, I have not carried any cash in my wallet for a long time; I have used only two credit cards pretty much everywhere for years now. I can simplify things I carry and track down where I spend money on banking sites that way; I pay the balances off and get rewards as "cashback" at the end of every month. Surely, I get cash from ATMs when it's necessary, which rarely happens. I've never lost a dollar since I don't carry it from the start – *having only one type of payment has made my life simpler*.

Some say consumers tend to spend more when they use credit cards, instead of cash. That may be true to many, but I personally haven't had that issue as far as I know. I spend probably $1,500 a month, including my condo HOA fee[8]. I haven't paid any type of late charges, fees or interest for decades; I do "get" interests and dividends from my savings and portfolio every month, though. I guess I am frugal and have control over money.

* * *

[8] $367 a month in 2023.

Whenever things don't go well, what I do first is *simplifying*; it clears things out. **Usually not spending money for a while works the best, according to my experience**; it makes life easier fast. Next, I usually stop checking sites I usually go to; use my phone less; eat or talk less. I just have to wait until bad things move away. I usually focus on basic things (e.g., paying bills) for a while without eating out or traveling around. Now it's February, 2023 and the Dow dropped 3,000 points in the past month; I expect we may get into a recession slowly; it's pointless to try to grab more money, compete excessively or move to a bigger house in situations like this. We can complicate things only when things are great. Maybe this is why I have only one child and decided not to expand my family, which I feel wise about; things have been rough in the past decade, including COVID; it won't get better any time soon. After all, I realize a minimal life makes me happy the most.

I think writing is an odd way to connect our minds to our sub-consciousness. If I get some ideas, I only know what to write in the first couple of sentences; then, I am occasionally surprised at how the entire paragraph ends. I end up with something I did not expect in the beginning. Psychologists suggest our subconsciousness determines 95% percent of our apparent behaviors; everything I wanted to express has been underground all along. Additionally, I think writing is a good way to organize and simplify floating thoughts.

Some people think doing more is a way to be happier or at least productive; nothing can be farther from the truth. I witnessed some insist on doing something without benefit or even creating troubles only to get out of boredom. For example, some play video games, not necessary for actual survival; their eyes get hurt eventually, so they need to visit an eye doctor; all those cost money, so they have to work longer; hence, their children don't see parents as often; the family become strangers and divorce happens – vicious cycles. While they have been through all those, their homes become more crowded with games, consoles, toys, eye medicines, divorce papers, etc. *They could have not done anything to begin with* and spent time with their children.

Whenever things go bad, I usually stop spending money for a week, month or quarter, depending how serious it is. I just do not spend anything other than APT rent (which is the condo association fee now) if I start that *period*; I pay utility bills as well, but that is about it. With no spending, we might have to skip some meals for a while, which is good for weight loss. We will eventually feel better and have more money in our pockets as a result. According to my experience, it should solve *problems other than money-related* as well in the end.

* * *

It was 2008 when I met the oldman Lester; I was single then and he was a customer of my store Cyb Knight. Out of nowhere, he successfully persuaded me to have a baby after a conversation; my daughter was born in 2010 afterwards. He has been single himself for life and I was 35 in 2008; then I had a lot of pressure to have a baby from my parents, who would be a grandchild for them. I recall the pressure intensified after I became 30. Nonetheless, my parents have always insisted on diverse things for me, which I hate. It was just baby pressure at that time. As a result, I just don't speak with them any more.

I thought that it was not reasonable to pressure myself to have a baby, only because I was old enough; then, I was single and broke. It could have been more understandable if my parents pushed me to make sufficient money to support myself; which I won't insist to my daughter. I have always thought my parents don't have common sense – they've never known the boundaries for what they can or cannot ask others. They were unpleasantly demanding people despite having some money. While Lester was not an ideal customer, he had visited my store for long. Accidentally, one day I found that he didn't have a kid; he said he could not have one. I was surprised and asked, "What do you mean you couldn't?"

That day, he told me a lot of things that I had not known. Until then, I thought only getting pregnant could be a problem. I learned not getting pregnant can also be an issue for the first time; I didn't realize some have a hard time getting conceived or adopting a child. He said he and his wife tried everything, but finally gave up completely after 40. I was approaching 40 fast then, whereas the store didn't make much profit.

I thought I needed a change to get out of the miserable destiny I was already in – being solo, impoverished and profitless from the business. In conclusion, having a child profoundly changed my life, while it was an unexpected addition in my family. I had to go through some sort of hell after my daughter was born; I guess it must have been very painful for her, too. All I can say now is there is a reason I decided not to have any more babies. I learned that simplification always made my life easier while addition did it harder.

* * *

**Summary**

1. Simplification is essential to be organized.
2. Stop spending money for a while makes our lives simpler fast.
3. I learned that addition always makes my life harder.

# 45

# Being Impulsive

*I don't write stories; I need to entangle ideas slowly.*
-Brad Kong

The richest person ever alive on Earth was John Rockefeller (1839 – 1937), who lived for 97 years. It's said that not only did he have a *calm temper*, but his heart beat was actually slower. I can say that the longer we stay composed, the more money we make. I think tranquil people are true winners in real lives; from my observation, they tend to be more achieving than others. Koreans are known for having hot tempers and many falsely believe it's a good thing: **Not necessarily.** I believe the more we get emotional, the more money we lose after all. The good news is I surmise we can strengthen our composure with practices, including meditation.

It is true that a lot of men don't know how to attract women, including myself. The popular relationship expert, Bob Rio, emphasized that uncertainty is the key. He explained sports games won't be fun if we know the final scores already; fans are thrilled since they don't know it yet. It could be the same for dates: Rio tipped that *women tend to think of a man* constantly *when she is not sure* of what he is thinking. A lot of guys shout his intentions too early; Rio suggested single men should stop *confessing* their feelings easily; **maybe they shouldn't do it at all,** as girls are not a catholic father.

Theoretically, these guys who suck at dating that way could be honest people; they may be straightforward businessmen who hate wasting time. The only problem is they don't really get the girl they want; Rio mentioned many end up with girls they've never been interested in: Why? The girl who failed to get attention from a man naturally has no clue about his intentions – he had nothing on her, to begin with. Ironically, that's the reason why she wonders about him ceaselessly, once she is into him. Those impatient guys never play with girls' minds, though; they usually get *impulsive* and lose.

* * *

*The 48 Laws of Power* by Greene says there was a woman named "Ninon Lenclos" in France in the 17th century; she had been a courtesan for life, so must have known about women's psychology better than anyone; she was 62 when she was consulting an aristocrat Marquis Sévigné, having struggle to pursuit a young countess. Lenclos suggested that Sévigné should keep some distance from the lady, first of all; she asked him to have a conversation with her: "We will be friends for now." Then, Lenclos planned ahead to make the countess jealous. She had Sévigné surrounded by other women at the parties; Lenclos explained women are interested in a man who is popular among girls. Next, she instructed Marquis to be *unpredictable*; sometimes he went to a party and sometimes he missed it out of the blue. Everything seemed to go right smoothly.

Then, suddenly, without informing Madam Lenclos, Marquis visited the countess' house one day. He decided to wrap things up his way; he did straight talk with the countess impulsively; he *confessed* how much he was in love. After that, unfortunately, the countess had not been available all the time whenever Marquis tried to see her. She allowed him to come in long later, but Marquis himself did not want it any more, by then. Sounds familiar? They ended up becoming acquaintances, after all.

Personally, I like *straightforward* people. Still, here is something we all need to know: *Waiting* is the key for attraction. I think all the methods Lenclos used were handy to make things happen quickly. Yet I assure you that **single women tend to be in love with the man who is genuinely interested in them eventually**; this is how human generations have continued over 6 million years; if it didn't work this way, we would have gone extinct long ago. Women's minds have adapted that way evolutionarily since it's impossible for every woman to get the *exact* man she wants biologically; that probability is like winning the lottery. From the DNA point of view, generations need to continue somehow despite this discrepancies of ideal types; I believe nature has changed her mind to adaptate flexibly.

The only problem is that a woman's mind changes slowly, which takes up to years. Throughout evolution, a female animal of human species has been in trouble, when she chooses a wrong partner. By instinct, she takes her time to watch and think – in fact, it's a life and death matter for all the female animals on Earth since so many male partners have killed them[9] throughout the history of billion years; police investigations and court sentences were created only recently. She may still marry a man with flaws, but she wants to know if these are affordable. While I took examples of relationships, being impulsive can make us lose other games than dating in life, too.

* * *

Being placid brings us profits as *fighting is a loss even for winners*. Calming my temper is something I have to try to acquire all the time. My father has been rather an explosive person – he got divorced in the end and made his two sons enemies. Which means I may have to go against my own temper inherited from parents. In my opinion, **the job of an investor is all about waiting**, which is called timing, occasionally; if we cannot be patient, we just don't make dough, as the right moment is available only once in a while. Rarely, we have to learn how to kill years, if not decades, wisely; I decided to write while waiting for chances, instead of doing anything wasteful. Self-publishing books only requires me to read and think, which does not cost me any money.

Simultaneously, I notice that I cannot write whenever I try to write a masterpiece; I guess I ought to write as if I am

[9] Almost all the males are bigger and stronger than females.

talking to a friend. I cannot squeeze ideas out of my brain; I need to wait until some come to me, which is important not to miss. **In that sense, the job of a writer is waiting as well;** in a broader view, *being successful* is all about *waiting patiently.* I trust those who can wait and do things step by step can achieve everything. I lost over $3,500 for a bad deal when I was impetuous in 2005; then I was 32 and it was right before leaving the terrible town of Buffalo for good. As I wrote before, I don't think we make money evenly throughout our lives; we lose some more earlier and make more later. It looks to take almost 18 years to learn the lesson: always staying serene.

I was a late college student in SUNY Buffalo, NY in 2005. eBay was big then and I was trying to make an income out of selling used items on it – starting with small stuff I didn't need at home, initially. Subsequently, I sold used video games I bought from a wholesaler who was a bit of a fraud; he was an Indian or Arab named Hassem and gave me unpopular sports titles though he lied these were popular; I was able to sell them all with a very slim margin, nonetheless. It was an era before I was able to tell popular titles, made up my mind to sell only games and open Cyb Knight in Chicagoland in 2006.

In 2005, one day, I saw a car with a sale sign in front of a house near my Cheektowaga apt: $3,000. It was a Mercury Cougar 2001 in white, looking fine outside. When I checked the price on eBay, these were listed at up to $6,000. All of sudden, I got excited, which was plainly stupid. When I think about it now, the car had been in the same spot for months; there must have been reasons why no one wanted it. Also, there was a reason why the trashy young owner, Justin, could not sell it on eBay on his own, either. But I wasn't sane. I was obsessed with the greed that I could make $3,000 profit out of one simple transaction. I think $3,000 in 2005 was like $6,000 in 2023. It was a big profit for a broke student who I was.

When I stopped at the house, the boy's mother came out. She took my phone number as her son, who was the car owner, was not there. I recall she was a nurse and single mother with two sons; her trashy older son drove the vehicle too roughly, who was about 22, a community college dropout and went out of the town frequently for any reason. Later, I learned that he was waiting to join the army in a few months. **I was too eager to make money and waited to close the deal no matter what, desperately.** I got a phone call from him about three days later and he said he can make it for $2,500. I met and handed him $2,500 cash even without a test drive or checking all documents – a huge mistake.

* * *

First of all, I found out that the used car didn't have a license plate; I was idiotic not to even question it. I was really out of my mind for a possible $3,000 profit. What made me crazy the most was the boy kept being unavailable to apply for the plate together as both old and new owners were needed in this case. I believe it took about a week to get a hold of him and we went to the DMV together to get the plate, finally. I still remember he kept smoking a cigar and said, "Life cannot be better than this," or something outside the DMV (WTF?).

Secondly, the condition of the car was way worse than I expected. Unnaturally, the outside looked close to new, which was what my potential buyers said later on, too. She didn't have a super high mileage as well, so I assume the boy must have driven her very badly. I recall he said to make a round trip to California on her; if I had a minute test driving, I would have walked away permanently. I spent an extra $500 on repairing it at a Meineke, which did not improve her condition very much.

Thirdly, I made a mistake not to tell the difference between "listing price" and "sold price" on eBay. We can list this Cougar for $6,000. But that is not the final sales price, but merely a suggestion in fact. Later, I learned a majority of Cougars sold much less than listing prices on eBay. Eventually, it was sold about $4,000 twice even though both buyers decided to walk away without paying me for different reasons. The driving comfort of the car was awful. I learned countless lessons out of the experience. All of these happened in 2005 when I was about to graduate from the college, so I ended up donating it to a Kidney Foundation before graduation in 2006. When I think about it now, that was the last mistake since I could have sold it for $500 to the junkyard; I needed some money to move out, anyway. For some reasons, nothing worked out and no one helped me in NY and I am glad I moved to Illinois as soon as I was done with the school.

A similar thing could have happened when I tried to buy a house in 2012. For some reason, I was obsessed with a three bedroom house in Roselle. Luckily, my wife blocked me at that time saying, "Will you buy a house even without a home inspection?" She had a solemn face, which quickly reminded me of what happened in Buffalo.

I didn't like all those people involved in the auto sales in 2005: the grungy boy, his mother and a stupid babysitter for the younger brother in the family who wrote a cunning contract for the auto sales, which was bad for me. I cannot believe his mother even paid for a babysitter since Justin did not want to take care of his younger brother while not doing anything – very useless. *I should have not missed all those negative signs* and gotten involved with these people from the start. But, in the end, *it was my avarice playing a major role* in getting into the trap.

Never get spontaneous if you need to win. We are living in an absurd society promoting rushing beyond necessity. We do not have to make ourselves hasty all the time. Some get into a "squeezing-time-out" pattern since they are too lonely. We need to keep composed only not to lose, after all.

* * *

**Summary**

1. The longer we stay calm, the more money we make.
2. Greed inside us is the most formidable enemy.

3. Waiting patiently can get us everything step by step in the end.

# 46

# Not Being a Good Spouse or Parent

It costs to be rude; being selfish is expensive.
-Brad Kong

Wiki shows Cameron Douglas, who is the son of the actor Michael Douglas, had been in prison for seven years; he was convicted for felony drug dealing. I read Michael said he wishes he would have spent more time with his son in an interview. Being a parent may be expensive and time consuming; yet I assume **not being a good parent can cost a fortune.** Nonetheless, just in my opinion, I wondered if Michael's marrying the younger actress, Zeta-Jones, and producing two more kids was truly necessary. Apparently, I felt he wound up having more things to worry about, after all.

As a head of household, I think it's important for me to leave my daughter and wife alone. If I don't say a thing, they don't offend me back, anyway (at least, not the way my parents did). If I keep over-concerning their lives, all of us may not end up living together under the same roof – living *separately* means paying more rent in a family, meaning an enormous loss. Nevertheless, I notice some drain more money by being assholes to their own families. From my perspective, the best thing I have done for my wife was letting her get pregnant only once. Not only did I make her less painful physically, I think I let her psychologically feel comfortable as well. She seemed to have a strong prejudice to having two children, originally; I gave her more than enough reason why she didn't have to. I still believe no one gets benefit out of me only because I have two children, instead of one.

First of all, I myself would have been more exhausted physically to take care of an extra baby if having another happened to us. Secondly, I might have spent twice more, while I get stressed out financially. I could have been in the situation to tutor two children face to face, which is tiring. I would have been in the condition to move out to a bigger house for a larger family, which can bring me a mortgage debt, which is a horrible loss with interest. In short, I am glad I didn't try something I feel against, only because of social stigma: "Having two kids is ideal!" Besides, having one less child is good for *chickens*, too. If a child is a meat eater, he or she can eat at least 100 birds during lifetime – pointless killing of 100 extra lives while humans get more crowded every day.

I believe that the best thing I can do for my daughter is just being alive and staying in the family. I don't think a child can grow better with extra tutorings or concerns from parents while I am too tired to do so. **Statistics show the chance a child without a father becomes a poor adult is *four times* higher than those with a**

**father.** I see why whenever I see what my wife is doing with money, including never buying a stock for her life. I will stay on Earth as long as possible, so I can pass my financial knowledge and little fortune to her – helping her stay far from the poverty line would be my gift.

* * *

As far as partnership goes, I don't think there will be a woman who can completely satisfy me overall; we can be fed up with any woman, regardless of whoever we married to, which is bad news, especially for men, but simply true. Please acknowledge it before getting married; whoever you marry, she won't be enough; there will always be a better woman; there will be continually a new girl you may find interesting in the future. In a sense, it's true for foods, TV channels, movies and everything else. The only difference is the marriage system will push us to stick to *one* woman for life; people may learn marriage is a sort of house arrest or home confinement after all. Still, if we accept that before marriage, we may be fine. So there is no joy in married lives at all? There will be, but it won't be like a chunk of happiness everyday as in some popular beliefs – far from it.

Do you know what kind of person divorce more? The rude probably do more in my opinion. Have you ever had an unpleasant coworker before? It's highly possible the person has been divorced already or about to, according to my experience. There was a Cuban Mexican cook I never liked in my culinary job; she was plainly impolite to dishwashers. I learned she was divorced three times; she had five kids with three different men, but no one ended up staying with her. Personally, I didn't even understand why those men made a baby with her, to begin with. **All I can say is that it costs a lot to be impertinent to others, especially our own families.** No one can know more about us than our families, so we can end up making our spouse or children complete enemies if we are no good.

Lately, I learned it costs about $13,000 for a lady to have her eggs frozen at a fertility clinic in 2023. It's a free country, but personally, I don't understand why some stick to leaving their own DNAs this much; technically, they leave only half of their DNAs to an offspring at most, since the other half is from a sperm; it seems doctors put so many needles on women's abdomens during the multi-step process. If a pregnancy can happen naturally, that is fine and I can take care of the baby. But I will never try super hard to go through multiple surgeries only to leave half of my DNAs after spending a chunk of money. Our planet has millions of orphans, so adopting one would be more beneficial for society if singles really want a child.

Still, sadly, I have to suggest parents need to be cautious about adoption; we never know where those children are exactly from. I heard some horror stories, including eventual murders after adoptions. Even after fostering a good kid, becoming a parent is a neverending hard job; **I admit that these people adopting kids and raising them responsibly are real-life angels.**

The other day, I read an article titled “IVF and Single Girl” by Dionne, a black writer who won three awards. I didn't know the entire IVF process is a major surgery, which costs over $26,000 to develop the eggs to be a baby, on top of separate freezing costs. Plus, it costs way more to raise the baby in the next 20 years after birth. I felt expending this much and going through pains only to be a parent of my own DNAs is like spending money on getting into prison. I recall my wife couldn’t get out of the house for years only to take care of my daughter; so many women gave up their entire careers; motherhood is at least like a home detention as far as I have observed. If it happens smoothly, I do it, but I will never try an extreme measure to make it happen. For the record, our daughter was born without much hassle. My wife and I could have had dozens of more kids biologically. However, I decided not to since it has been so hard for me physically and financially in the past decades; Earth has been getting more overpopulated since then.

* * *

There is something a man needs to be aware of; apparently, there are girls (especially Latinas, according to my experience) getting attracted to mature men, particularly at work; they don't seem to care if he is married or not. Some may think I am crazy if I mention this, but let me be honest with you: I am glad I am not super-rich or handsome enough to attract those females; they may be young now, but we all know that they will get fat and ugly soon. Some successful men unluckily wound up having messy relationships, divorce lawyers, alimonies and a bunch of extra kids they do not enjoy rearing. Some think these rich men having married multiple times are plain fools, but there are wicked young lasses who know how to persuade them to tie the knot again. As their incomes depend on men, gold diggers have professional skill to make men insane and let them sign a deal absolutely disadvantageous for the groom. I am glad I am not a desirable target for them, to begin with.

Greed can make our own child an enemy. Sadly, I have not spoken with my parents for over a decade. Their unreasonable demands, which do not benefit anyone apparently, never stopped, so I had to cut them off despite their wealths. I witnessed this type of issue is especially noticeable in Korea. Culturally, there are a lot of *education fanatic parents* in the nation; many spend a fortune on their children's tuitions, which is a frequent waste, and push them crazily to study. They don't do that to make their children happy or mature; they just want their children to get better grades and jobs eventually. As a parent myself, I would say it's disgusting to consider the future income from our own children – these form sick relationships and I know many end up as tragedies. Having a good relationship is not always about money. Yet, I strongly believe being a pleasant one, especially with my own family, is a way to accumulate wealth faster.

* * *

### Summary

1. We don't have to try super hard to create our own family.
2. Being a good person in the family is important in every sense, which saves a ton of money, incidentally.
3. Unnoticeably, being an asshole is an efficient way to get broke.

# 47

# Pressure to Spend Money

*Be comfortable sitting on money.*
-Brad Kong

As I mentioned briefly in the prologue, Jack Whittaker was a construction businessman in Putnam County, WV; he was known as the winner of a lottery jackpot of $315 millions in 2002. It shows he was already a millionaire with a net worth of $17 M before the big winning – a millionaire won a huge lottery! Ironically, a series of unfortunate events happened to him for no apparent reason after his win. First of all, a boy named Tribble, who was the boyfriend of Whittaker's granddaughter Brandi Bragg, was found dead of drug overdose in Whittaker's home in 2004; three months later, Brandi herself was also found deceased in the property of a male friend; it shows that cocaine and methadone were found in her body at 17.

Subsequently, Ginger Bragg, who was the mother of Brandi and Whittaker's daughter, was also found expired at 42 in Daniels, WV in 2009; the police suspected the cause was OD again. Then, Whittaker's home in Bland County, VA, was reported to be on fire in 2016. Finally, Mr.Whittaker himself passed away following a long illness in 2020. It was seen that he had frequented casinos and strip clubs; I guess lack of sleep and disorganized lifestyle might have brought him a little early demise at 72.

Seemingly, Whittaker had been generous enough to give a lot of money to the lottery ticket seller, his family members and others; that's how some of them bought a large quantity of drugs, to begin with. **There are always people who cannot sit on their money cozily.** Believe it or not, spending itself is labor in a sense. Couldn't he have lived off the interests out of the fortune for decades and pass it to children when he dies? He might have lived longer in frugality, as he passed away in early 70s. And that's what I am doing now.

In case you win a fortune, my suggestion is holding it for a year without doing anything. Just put the entire amount in a CD or ETF and get some interest out of it (up to 19% a year from an ETF like TLTW). *Most people get strong urges to waste a windfall only in the beginning.* Sooner or later, you may get into the *next phase*: You may be upset if you do not have it in your hands; your point of view on net worth shifts – reasonable spendings starts only after that point. I think decency matters since it attracts people by making them feel better; it makes the owners lose less money, which matters more for the rich since they own more things to lose. When we insist on living a decent lifestyle, we waste less. For example, some rich people choose to spend time in the library, instead of the red light district in Bangkok. We get true respect while we stay in wealth longer that way.

There is a difference between decency and snobbery, though; decency gives good feelings to others while snobbery doesn't; decency is from modesty whereas condescension comes from the low quality showing off. Mukesh Ambani, who is the chairman of Reliance, built a $1 B house called Antilia in Mumbai, India; his house looks like a tasteless square tall skyscraper to me. I had been raised in a rectangular condo like many Koreans did and felt I was standing in front of people uncomfortably at home. Regardless, it's not a decent thing to do when half of Indians don't have proper toilets. There is no way we can live happily alone; I would have donated some money for building infrastructures if I were him. Stupidly, *he only made other Indians enemies* for nothing.

* * *

Michael Hartono is a Chinese Indonesian billionaire in Kudus, Indonesia; his net worth is estimated to be $20 B in 2023 – the richest man in Indonesia in the last 11 years consecutively, according to *Forbes*. Weirdly, a photo showing him eating alone at a modest restaurant went viral all over on social media in 2019. The cafe owner said Hartono has been a regular for a long time since he sold food on the street. He mentioned this billionaire is a simple guy who didn't mind eating on the street.

I am not particularly respecting him, but I felt a bit of decency – good feelings, modesty or a sort of attraction. I believe this is why Gorat's, which is the magnate Buffett's favorite restaurant, is also popular in America. **Being decent doesn't cost any money**; it often *saves* money in fact. Nevertheless, I believe it's the most important asset the affluent need to carry – I like to think I've been decent enough to be a writer, instead of spending all my investment profit on sports cars. It's nice to spend time thinking and studying freely without getting financial pressure: Maturity and decency make our wealth sustainable.

There was the *Lollapalooza* music festival in downtown Chicago the other day; I just went downtown for my walking exercise, so it was a surprise to me. I saw endless parades of girls in bikini tops and jean shorts, which seemed to be uniforms for female audiences. I saw some black market sellers selling *wristbands*, which were *admission ticket* to the venue Grant park; they said these were $300 each, but I found that the original price was $125; I saw some men selling T-shirts having obscene phrases for $20 each; they shouted to pedestrians, but I did not see anyone buying one for hours. Frankly, for some reason, I couldn't really detect a pretty looking girl among the crowds that day – mostly they looked cheesy and their clothes looked cheap. I did not like the blasting sounds from distant speakers or enjoyed the blazing sun; I did not have money for the ticket, yet also didn't feel I would enjoy the festival; it could have been nothing but a pain for me.

I went to Chinatown on my kick scooter *right after* Lollapalooza. Unfortunately, the town was even worse; it had a sort of summer festival as well, and I wasn't sure where all these bad smells and *cheap feelings* were from. I know I was supposed to feel lucky to catch two festivals within a day, but that wasn't what I felt. Just low life feelings that I had never felt from Andersonville or Schaumburg. I have been to plenty of art festivals as well (e.g., Arlington Heights, Oak Brook mall, etc), but this was the first time I felt something like this. Most fairs had brought me reasonably decent feelings, but I felt like I am the only human among monkeys.

After pondering over why overnight, I conclude decency comes from something beyond materials. An example is education; we just have to read books and think enough daily to give high quality feelings to others. There is a word "pariah capitalism" in Korea; I can translate it to "bum capitalism" in America. Some may be rich, but they spend all on drinking, gambling, shopping or prostitution; they just don't give a positive feeling to others. I think the recent economic boom has produced a lot of these, especially in China; I hope they will mature too as time goes on, instead of focusing mostly on the basic instincts.

* * *

In my opinion, the most stupid out of all desires humans have is *consumption* desire – the impulse to spend money on no visible ground. Do you know how we can make a $1 M mansion into a cheap slum? Buy 1,000 items from the Dollar Tree and spread them in the house. That will do even after spending money. Weirdly, I had so much of the urge when I lived in Ithaca, NY in 1999, which was a small college town with a population of 50,000 then. The city was surrounded by layers of mountains and no major highway went through the city. I always felt suffocated as if I was locked in a broom closet.

I think I spent more money than ever in my life while I studied at Cornell in 1999; I received so much complaint of spending too much from my father. However, I was shocked that his complaint stopped almost immediately as soon as I moved into Buffalo in 2000; part of the reason was the living cost there was much cheaper than that of Ithaca; in fact, it is cheaper than any city in America. And my suffocation magically disappeared after I moved into the big city, Chicago later in 2006; the living cost of Windy city is not that bad even compared with that of Buffalo. Some people may be astonished at this simple truth: We do not have to do anything except eat and breathe. There is no animal on Earth born with ambition, greed or personal agenda other than humans; in a sense, these are the things making us uniquely painful. Everyone dies and **no one will get reward in heaven since he or she worked harder than others during lifetimes.**

We have the right to live freely unless we bother others. We don't have to pursue Personal Legend as Coelho suggested in *The Alchemist*. **It's a problem that people keep pressuring us to have an idea that we have to do something** – we don't! We do not have to go on a blind date since others get married. We don't have to go to India to see and broaden our knowledge – some wound up being dead by crime or contaminated food. You can trust me that we do not have to do anything. So stop checking Facebook and take some breaks.

When we get a windfall suddenly, we will feel pressured to spend it; sometimes, people actually can make profit out of stocks or inherit fortunes. According to my experience, the heavy compulsion comes only in the beginning. If we can pass a year without spending, we can keep it forever. Please trust me that we need money later on; we are in a society where we can use dough everyday. After a year, we won't *feel* we have the bonanza any more – no sense since it's marinated and submerged in our lives already. I am not saying we need to be greedy to keep more; **I am saying we don't have to waste it unnecessarily only by impulse.**

* * *

## Summary

1. If you happen to get a fortune, don't spend it right away – hold it for a year.
2. A year later, you may be angry if you don't have the initial amount any more.
3. Spending pressure is temporary, so we need to pass some time wisely.

# 48

# Not Getting up Early

*If you want to make life better instantly,*
*sleep an hour early tonight.*
-Brad Kong

There is a rock star *inspiration promoter* named Kim in Korea. I still remember she said one thing: "My mom used to wake up extremely early. She always said we survive as long as we get up early, even though we are destitute." I think keeping early hours is a way to make our life efficient instantly without spending extra. Staying late *usually* means *wasting* more – probably less than half of people stay late to work or study more. Many stay late to do something unnecessary or even harmful.

How do we know if we live a fine life or not? I think the instant way is checking our weights – an easy but the most effective visual indicator. We are living in an era to get fat easily; foods are available at low costs everywhere. If you are skinny by chance, you are probably living a fine life; probably you won't live as social pressures push you blindly; most likely you are living with your own ideas. Why? Being skinny is only possible after rejecting myriads of foods. Besides, if you are lean, you are probably intelligent enough to be conscious about being healthy from a medical point. As a result, you won't waste a lot on medical bills in the future as well: So what can we do when we are *not slim enough*?

Oddly, *I learned sleeping early is the fastest way to lose weight,* which worked out for me. Physiologists explain that a hormone called "Ghrelin" comes out in our bodies after 10:00 PM every night, which is known to cause extreme hunger in the middle of night. That is why those late night restaurants are unexpectedly crowded. **I think it's better for us to sleep before hunger strikes us.** Wiki also depicts, "The level of ghrelin gradually increases from midnight to dawn." When we sleep through, we cannot devour any food overnight. Besides, it informed me that our body burns fat while we are sleeping, which accelerates weight loss.

Physiologically, it's said a hormone doing the opposite function of ghrelin is "leptin," which makes us feel full. It shows it only comes out 20 minutes after starting eating a meal in our body. Since it does not have any specific time of the day to release, *theoretically* it may be a good idea to skip dinner and sleep early to lose maximum weight (I don't do that as I usually eat dinner). I believe there is not much calorie consumption during the night as we don't move much, physically.

Being skinny by some harmful methods (e.g., smoking) does not count for living a fine life, though. When I worked at the nursing home, there was an Italian smoker girl who was skinny. When I checked her Facebook, both of her parents were obese. She was the only white among diet aids (mostly Mexicans and Indians) and poorer than any coworker there; her parents lost their house by foreclosure in 2010 and her entire family has lived in a rental APT since then. Maybe I am describing her horribly since she was rude to me. Nonetheless, I felt like the smoking of everyone in that family, including parents and two daughters, had brought them hefty indigence.

There is a strict rule I suggest to single guys for dating – no fat or talkative women! Talkative ladies will continuously distract others as I've never liked a chatty person, regardless of gender. Perhaps I am writing this way since the girl above was a wordy smoker having fat parents; she had given me pain without getting any benefit for herself. Another barometer to measure our conditions can be how much balance we keep in our bank accounts, to be honest, as money doesn't accumulate automatically. I assume we can use hormones and biorhythm patterns for our advantages. If you want to get wealthier and skinnier, sleeping early is a costless starting point.

* * *

For some reasons, I notice our societies are built easier for early risers; this is true for every country I've been to, yet particularly accurate in Northern Europe, including Denmark. Even in Chicago, when we check the public transportation schedules, we can see it immediately; for example, there is a bus called "Pace 600 express" connecting to the Blue Line subway from Northwestern center behind Woodfield mall; its schedule starts at 5:00 AM everyday, but finishes as early as 7:00 PM on Sat; there is no bus at all in that huge terminal after that. When we actually check the open hours of anything from libraries to malls, we can find everything is set easier for early birds and harder for night owls.

Sleeping early can help us cut out any bad habits from an angle. For instance, if we want to quit drinking, we can start it by sleeping early. Not many people drink during the day time. When it's dark outside, we can just sleep, so we can save electricity in the worst case. Personally, I struggle to decrease the internet hours. I notice I do more pointless browsing after evening. I guess I will sleep by 9:00 PM, so I can write more early in the morning. While keeping early hours makes people wealthier in general, I have not been an early riser by nature, frankly. Nevertheless, I found out I can do more things in those a few hours early in the morning.

* * *

I happened to watch a documentary about "Angola Three" in 2005; the film was about three African American prison inmates held for decades in solitary confinement. A Jewish reporter interviewed one of them, and he said he was falsely accused of murder which happened at 1:00 AM when outside. As soon as I heard that, a strange idea hit me: "**If he was sleeping that time, would he have been involved in the crime?**" Occasionally, a chain of unfortunate events starts from one little bad habit. Then, I was young and used to go out any time I wanted at night; I remember I started sleeping much earlier after watching the interview. Nonetheless, I had a minor car accident after moving to IL in 2011; a taxi driven by a young Indian guy, who seemed exhausted by overworking, hit my butt hard while I tried to cross the road in Downtown Chicago. It happened at about 10:00 PM on a Saturday night. Walking around downtown then was fun, but not necessary to me. Maybe I am alive now since I don't do that any more after the accident.

I believe most can save a heavy amount of money only by changing their life cycles a little. Imagine there are identical twins: A and B. Suppose A wakes up at 5:00 AM and sleeps at 9:00 PM; B wakes up at 10:00 AM and sleeps at 2:00 AM; both are awake for the same 16 hours a day. Imagine both make $100,000 a year and it has been like this in the past twenty years. Who do you believe has saved more? I think A saved *five times* more than B: Why?

First of all, there are less places available to spend money when we get up and sleep too early. Where can we really go at 5:00 AM? Not that many money sucking businesses are open that hour. Maybe we can go to the gym, but possibly we save more from medical bills by doing exercise. On the contrary, when you sleep at 2:00 AM, there are so many bars and restaurants open till late night. We can also go to strip clubs or casinos; alcohol brings DUI tickets, legal disputes, violences, harassment or other hefty bills. I still believe people can stay out of countless troubles only by sleeping early at home.

* * *

## Summary

1. When we are not sure what to do to get out of destitution, sleeping early is an easy way to start.
2. Going to bed early makes us lose weight naturally.
3. A lot of troubles happen overnight while we do not notice – all of which we can avoid only by sleeping at home.

# 49

# Living for Harmful Satisfactions

*Satisfaction and happiness are two different things.*
-Brad Kong

There is an American romance writer named Steel; she has been divorced five times and has nine children (one died of suicide, unfortunately). Seemingly, she has lived a productive life, including publishing over 500 novels. Oddly, I found out her second husband was a prison inmate who she interviewed once in Lompoc, CA; she married him in 1975 even after he returned to jail on robbery and rape charges from 1974; it shows she eventually divorced him in 1978 after having multiple miscarriages. I think it's important to get addicted to a relationship. Love can be everything. Or it's merely a hormone interaction, which rushes us to produce more offspring. For the same reason, I think we shouldn't let our successes blind us to go too far.

My favorite Buddhist monk[10] once said, "There is no desire lasting forever." Even though we want something badly, if we believe it doesn't help, I think we should let time pass a while without doing it; maybe we won't want

[10] Pomnyun

it soon. I used to eat lots of Chicago dogs in different joints in 2021; I don't want any of those any more; I even feel disgusted by it, maybe because it's fatty food; personally, once a craving is gone, I find I don't want a specific menu forever. I guess the similar thing goes for dating. Maybe we should let a partner go if things do not work out well; it's possible that the person may not be as fantastic as we are imagining now.

I often feel the poor may be disrespected not because of lack of money, but because of being bothersome. Humans are not like plants; it's not that we don't move only because they don't have a job. By nature, people move, regardless of making money or not. When we do it in a constructive way, we can end up having sufficient one way or another; at least, we may stay above the poverty line. Being broke despite all those movements means having lived in wasteful ways; these usually bother others, which lowers the productivity of a society over all; some become a cancer of a community, too. We never get paid for annoying others, which is why some never get respect.

* * *

I don't think we can buy decency; having money helps us not downgrade our quality of lives, though. For example, personally, I have never felt a huge decency from Trump – all I feel is materialistic greed. **In a sense, "going for money all the time" is the attitude of a slave**; some may be rich, but they are still slaves. I think we can give a decent feeling only when we don't show off wealths; maturity must come along to emit decency. I was passing by Chinatown Chicago the other day; there were an array of massage parlors, so I opened a door only to check out the prices. Weirdly, a Chinese old man was standing virtually naked in the middle of the shop and hid quickly as soon as he saw me. I felt sickened – yucky – and left the town, which just didn't look the same after that. The man must have some money as shady massage can be a pure waste, but certainly not honorable. I am sure that not every Chinese is like that, but I guess I learned some lessons of what I will do.

I think buying fake luxury goods or getting vaginal surgery as in the book *When life gives us Lululemons* only makes us look cheap even after spending money; talking about TV soaps or celebrities puts a low price tag on us, while talking about books or speaking a foreign language puts pricey tags. Wearing a thong in the public pool or Chicago riverwalk didn't look attractive (some women); catcalling women or having too low standards on them is distasteful (men). Conclusively, I guarantee you that we will never buy decency with money.

* * *

***Not* reading a book is a guaranteed way to get penurious;** we can absorb other people's life lessons within hours by reading; we can advance fast as it might have taken twenty years for the writers to get those lessons. I just finished the book *Nomadland* the other day; shamelessly, I confess this is my first book in English that I finished *completely*. I found it for $2 at the clearance section of a Half priced book store; it was boring, but I thought I would finish a book completely at least *once* in my life. I have a habit to read some parts of books and move on to another; a Korean professor said it is ok, though, which is the reason why there are *contents* and *indexes*.

The book made me realize there are hidden *houseless* people in America. As the author admitted, a *houseless* is practically a "homeless"; I know some try to describe van life as "a cool life with freedom." But the reality is no one can sleep comfortably in a vehicle; a car can go too hot or freezing fast; the van dwellers have to worry which restroom they can use next time. For some reason, almost all living full-time in a van or RV are white Americans; many are old but it shows about one third of them had been wealthy when they were younger. **I also learned that virtually all of them had mortgage problems.**

My next book to read would be "Body" by Bryson; it looks thick, but I found it is *easier* to read than *Nomadland*. Personally, I hate people trying to write in a *hard* way; some don't give clear meaning *intentionally*, which is horrible. Also there are writers using rare words on purpose or twist grammar for artistic value; I *detest* them. I like Schopenhauer since his books are clear to read. There was a popular Korean professor named Ma, who was well-known for easy writing. He was the youngest professor of Yonsei University, which is an "Ivy league" in Korea; I read his motto was "*writing as easy as possible.*" I understood that he suffered from snobs enjoying hiding meanings arrogantly; some may think it is a way of showing off knowledge, but I think it is wasteful. Fictive languages were invented for us to communicate 70,000 years ago; it was not emerged to torture people.

Schopenhauer was the professor at the University of Berlin and Bryson is a former Chancellor of Durham University. I love those extremely educated ones writing in easy fashions. I am nobody now, but this would be my principle in writing: easy, simple and clear. Besides, I believe this is the only way I can sell more books since I expect non-native English speakers to read those. I have been a full-time writer since 2022 and wondered how I can be better. Here's my conclusion: Reading is the critical prerequisite; I may read 8 hours a day. Other books bring me more ideas; I can summarize other books, translate hard meanings and add my opinion; readers can get multiple books this way. I assume my book will be thicker as I read more. As a result, I hope this series will be full of quality points from my brain and other masterpieces.

* * *

Some say that we are living in the age of YOLO or "Be here now." Fine but, weirdly, I feel our society is changing to focus more on *instant satisfaction.* In a sense, the more we focus *on* now, the farther we may be from wealth since saving funds is not the most beneficial thing we can do for today. I bought a new Dell desktop package in 2022. It was a $550 deal with everything included: a new monitor, PC with Windows 11, keyboard, mouth, etc. I bought the same deal from it sixteen years ago in 2006 and had used it well for decades. So I did not expect any trouble: What can be wrong with a brand new PC, anyway? And, technically, I guess that Dell did not do anything wrong this time, too; they made a new PC combo at a low price and delivered it quickly with free shipping. I was amazed at the order processing speed and happy on the day it arrived.

Then, my itching eye problem started about three weeks after I started using it. I had used only an old flat screen 15" monitor in the past 18 years. But there must have been some technological advancements; Dell shipped a wide 24" high definition monitor with HD cable this time. I have lived without a TV for a couple of decades now for my mental peace and meditation; I have avoided movie theaters and Blu-ray players as well. I noticed this high definition monitor killed my eyes seriously. This may not be Dell's fault; I assume that they developed new tech, accordingly. Here are 11 ways I figured out how to save our eyes from frying by using sharp monitors.

1. If you own a Dell brand monitor, you will see five buttons right below the screen, which usually are the same

for other monitors. The first button from the left is preset modes – choose "Comfort view."

2. Raise the contrast to 80%; letters would be more visible from far distances. We can place ourselves farther from the screen this way.

3. Make the brightness a little bit darker than your surroundings. I have an LG smartphone and it has an automatic brightness adjustment function under display. When I turn it on in my computer room, it shows that the recommended brightness is 51%; I set the brightness of the desktop monitor to 50%. I had thought that the dark screen was good by mistake. It is like when we get into a dark room, we tend to put some pressure in our eyeballs to search for things: **Pressuring our eyes for long can give us headaches.**

4. I feel better with my old VGA cable than the new HDMI one although both are 1080p.

5. Make the sharpness up to 40%; the preset was 50%, which I lowered a little bit.

6. Avoid the blue background on the Windows start screen; I notice that anything blue hurts my eyes more.

7. Download free Magic eye 3D images and use one of them as a background image. They actually improve vision by changing focus inside our eyes.

8. Buy a blue light prevention glass, which is only $5 on Amazon.

9. Take a look around every twenty minutes.

10. **Choose a matte screen monitor,** instead of glossy; I didn't have a choice for a combo deal. I found my old Dell monitor was way more matte than the new one. I suspect Dell added glossy for gamers as I found Xbox gaming features in Windows 11. I turned all those off as they made my computer slow.

11. Get rid of other HDTV or Gaming monitors from home; don't bring a smartphone outside to fry your eyes more. TVs are designed only for maximum visual effects, which will kill our eyes off in the end.

Finally, I switched these two monitors and have used my old Dell monitor for almost 2 years now.

* * *

## Summary

1. Too many people waste money on instant but harmful satisfaction.
2. Those will hurt our eyes and health at high speed.
3. Cut most out – enough is enough!

# 50

# Not Realizing Money Drain

*What makes a castle collapse is not a missile*
*– it's a mouse hole.*
-Brad Kong

Yesterday, I watched a documentary about "lonely death," which is spreading in Korea. A lot of adults are living alone in micro apts in the country – unmarried, separated or divorced – and they die alone, occasionally. It focused on one lady in her 40s and I confirmed there is alcoholism behind all the suicide by depression, including this one. After all, it's not that poor people commit suicide – more likely, it's alcoholics committing it after becoming destitute. It showed the lady ran away from her family after junior high, which is rare. I don't know what made her, but I felt sorry since I have a daughter myself. It's unimaginable if I cannot see her again like that.

I finally got my molar tooth extracted in 2022. It has been the only tooth I have lost until the age of 50. I struggled to save it for the last 4 years, but it was just too late. After losing it, I found out leaving an infected tooth in my mouth had been quite dangerous. It shows up to 40% of people used to die because of an abscessed tooth before the invention of antibiotics in 1928. Even nowadays, so many people end up in the emergency room because of infections caused by periapical tooth abscess. Pulling a tooth out was *not* as painful as I expected after getting *four* shots of anesthesia; besides, an infected tooth tends to come out easily since our bodies don't want it. The entire process cost me only $208 (2022). If you have chronic pain because of a tooth, my suggestion is just remove it. Subsequently, we can decide whether we live without it or have a dental implant. I triple assure it's never a good idea to keep a source of incurable infection in our heads; it shows some die because that moves to their brain. Little things are not little, which can kill us. We have to watch out for any little leakage in our finances as well.

A Korean doctor claimed fasting 12 hours a day is critically important; he explained eating continuously makes our hormones less potent and lower metabolisms; we gain weight as a result. Some hormones have a function to burn out foods (e.g., leptin); these don't work effectively when we keep being full. Skipping a meal for 12 hours sounds hard, but it's not; many of us sleep 8 hours a day overnight, so actual time for us to fast consciously is 4 hours. Nonetheless, I think lots of people do not realize that it costs a *fortune* to eat, to begin with. When I lost a lot of weight in 2019, I was surprised that my money kept accumulating without having better income. I am trying to establish a habit of eating one meal a day for life. **It's for health reasons, but I calculated I can save $ millions that way in**

**the next 50 years.** *Eating less* is a wise way to save money while making ourselves healthier; personally, I've never dated a fat woman not because they don't look good, but they don't make a sensible choice.

* * *

The electricity bills were the problem when I had my video game store in 2009. The business itself was ok in the beginning in 2006, but I was able to see a loss after three years in 2009. I used to pay up to $300 for electricity a month for that small store of 900 sf; in the first a few months, I used to turn on lights and aircon all night even though no one was working there; I thought it would be an ad since people can notice my store during the nights, which was a mistake. When I actually checked it, those electricity bills of $3,600 a year were about 3 months rent in 2009. **Little leak was not little**; a tiny hole in a water tank can drain all out in a week. We always have to look out for a little waste; I know it can make a huge difference in the end.

I suspect the biggest money drain in America could be *lawn care* for houses. CA has had a severe drought since June 2022, which could be intensifying as summer barely started yet. I saw on the news that Lake Mead is drying up fast; people can get up to a $1,200 fine for watering their own lawn during the day there. I live in IL, and saw some watering their lawn this evening. Suddenly, a question hit me: What do all lawns do for houses, exactly? *Nothing,* really. I doubt they produce more oxygen; it has no significant function except covering the grounds, which is true for every plant. Sometimes, I have wondered what would happen if every house planted corn in their front yards. Apparently, it can be a better choice: Corns are tall plants, so they can cover our windows for privacy; we can harvest corns to eat, which is good for our kidneys; most importantly, they will provide way more biodiversity than lawns for other lives: More ants, spiders, insects, etc; Earth will have more lives. I think it's more productive than wasting water on lawns.

There was a nasty troll on a Korean site. In fact, there are such brats on every site: someone who never contributes anything, but always leaves bad comments on others' postings; for no apparent reason, that garbage had done those for years; the site was about job info, by the way. One thing I noticed was he had *a huge mortgage debt*. He claimed to have bought a $600,000 house with a 30-year mortgage – the total he owes is over $1,000,000, including $400,000 interest. Plus, he said he had a couple of luxury cars with car loans. Also, he had HDTVs and other pricey items with credit card debts. Conclusively, he has all sorts of debts: mortgages, car loans, card debts, etc. He said his wife has no job (of course, no professional lady marries such an idiot), so I assumed he must have been in deep trouble. I believe nasty comments reflected his misery.

Here is my question to him: "You will not be OK if you see a $5 unclear charge on the supermarket receipt. **But**

**how come you are fine with a $400,000 extra charge for the same house?"** I am sure some of his neighbors must have bought their houses in full – as high as 50% of them in 2022. Why is he satisfied with this? Or is it vice versa? He lived in a trashy way, so he ended up being like that? His logic was he could use some of the money for investing, instead of putting all in housing. He said "anyone" can make 7% a year only by putting some in the S&P 500 index fund: *Nonsense.*

First of all, the $400,000 interest loss by the mortgage is a "confirmed" loss; making money out of investment is merely "hope." **Hope is not an established profit:** When we make a profit, it is a profit, which should come with a "settled" x amount of dollars. Secondly, we don't make money out of S&P 500 funds all the time, which dropped significantly in 2022. Anyone who invested in those funds in 2020 must have lost 30% then.

* * *

Personally, I do not see anything wrong with purchasing a moderate house with a mortgage, which is technically not a gain, but an acceptable loss. I just didn't like the troll's attitude. It is reasonable if he shuts up and tries to pay off the mortgage ASAP. Who knows if he loses only $100,000, instead of $400,000 that way? **It is never a good idea to be in debt too long.** If you see $30 more on the electricity bill this month, you will try to figure out why that happened. If you see a $5 extra charge you don't understand on a receipt at Target, you will ask for a manager. But, strangely, a lot of people seem to be OK with extra $400,000 on their houses.

Some may think it is fine since others are doing it, too. When you think about it, *it is not really a matter of trend by population.* Even if 99% of people in the world have mortgages, it could be a saving if you do not have one. This is a personal gain and loss issue; it does not matter whether others do it or not. I don't blame people only because they have mortgages. I just thought it's *sinful* that someone doesn't admit his loss and acts nastily to others. I learned that nasty repliers always do that, regardless of content. Maybe pointing out their massive debts was a way I could attack them back on the site. If I were them, I would be depressed not to write anything online; I just didn't know what's wrong with those.

* * *

## Summary

1. Little loss is not little - check how much you can lose a year, instead of a month.
2. It is OK to have a mortgage. Don't insist it's a better deal than full cash payment – trolls are stupid.
3. Using money for investment, instead of paying off a house is risky – *wish* is not a profit!

# Author's Note

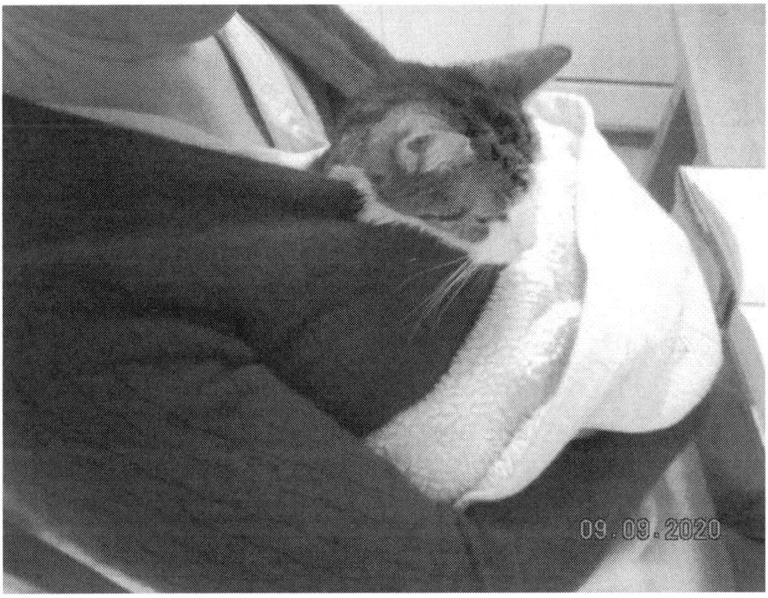


Congratulations: I truly appreciate you finishing my book until the end. The cat in the photo is Yang (Oscar) who I mentioned in Chapter 30 of *UnBrokable* III*; it was taken only a few days before he passed away. We had cherishable memories, but he couldn't get over the blood cancer in the end.

I was born and raised in South Korea and immigrated to America in my 20s; that was 24 years ago since it's 2023 now. In the beginning, I failed getting accepted to prestigious Ivy league schools although SUNYat Buffalo is great. Then I graduated from college with a 2.6 GPA by 2005, so I decided not to go to graduate school. Instead, I started my own business, but it wasn't very successful for 8 years. Subsequently, my career at the nursing home also didn't work out as I planned even though I won two certificates during the 7 years; now I try to be a writer.

If you believe this book can be helpful to others and have a minute to spare, ***I would appreciate a rating;*** your help in spreading the word will be grateful. *I do read all the reviews myself and use them to improve writing.* Reviews from readers like you make a difference; please let me know what you think. I sincerely wish my best luck to you!

# Book Club Discussion

1. What is the best reason you can agree with the author?

2. What is the reason you have least agreeable with the author?

3. What other reasons can you suggest?

4. What would you believe makes a person poor?

5. What can we do to improve our finances?

6. Who is Brad Kong and why is he a genius writer?

Let me know what you think of on Amazon reviews!

Made in the USA
Monee, IL
08 November 2026

67375665R00059